21st Century
Junior Library

TALKING ABOUT RACISM

AnneMarie McClain
and Lacey Hilliard

Topics to Talk About

Published in the United States of America by Cherry Lake Publishing Group
Ann Arbor, Michigan
www.cherrylakepublishing.com

Reading Adviser: Beth Walker Gambro, MS, Ed., Reading Consultant, Yorkville, IL
Book Designer: Jen Wahi

Photo Credits: Cover: © Pixel-Shot/Shutterstock; page 5: © DNF Style/Shutterstock; page 6: © fizkes/Shutterstock; page 7: © Jacob Lund/Shutterstock; page 8–9: Africa Studio/Shutterstock; page 10 (left): © Natalie Osipova/Shutterstock; page 10 (right): © Rawpixel.com/Shutterstock; page 11: © mae_chaba/Shutterstock; page 12–13: © iofoto/Shutterstock; page 14: © LightField Studios/Shutterstock; page 15 (top): © Pixel-Shot/Shutterstock; page 15 (bottom left): © JR-50/Shutterstock; page 15 (bottom right): © Ground Picture/Shutterstock; page 16: © szefei/Shutterstock; page 18: © fizkes/Shutterstock; page 19: © BGStock72/Shutterstock; page 20 (left): © Rido/Shutterstock; page 20 (right): © Pressmaster/Shutterstock; page 21: © voyata/Shutterstock

Library of Congress Cataloging-in-Publication Data

Names: Hilliard, Lacey, author. | McClain, AnneMarie, author.
Title: Talking about racism / written by Lacey Hilliard and AnneMarie McClain.
Description: Ann Arbor, Michigan : Cherry Lake Publishing, [2023] | Series: Topics to talk about | Includes bibliographical references and index. | Audience: Grades 2-3 | Summary: "How do we talk about racism? This book breaks down the topic of racism for young readers. Filled with engaging photos and captions, this series opens up opportunities for deeper thought and informed conversation. Guided exploration of topics in 21st Century Junior Library's signature style help readers to Look, Think, Ask Questions, Make Guesses, and Create as they go!"– Provided by publisher.
Identifiers: LCCN 2022039652 | ISBN 9781668919323 (hardcover) | ISBN 9781668920343 (paperback) | ISBN 9781668923009 (pdf) | ISBN 9781668921678 (ebook)
Subjects: LCSH: Racism—Juvenile literature.
Classification: LCC HT1521 .H46 2023 | DDC 305.8–dc23/eng/20220822
LC record available at https://lccn.loc.gov/2022039652

Cherry Lake Publishing would like to acknowledge the work of the Partnership for 21st Century Learning, a network of Battelle for Kids. Please visit http://www.battelleforkids.org/networks/p21 for more information.

Printed in the United States of America
Corporate Graphics

CONTENTS

LET'S TALK ABOUT RACISM

Your race or ethnicity is a part of who you are. Everyone is part of at least one racial or ethnic group. Do you know your race or ethnicity? Some people have more than one.

People with the same race may have the same skin color or culture. Culture is the way a group of people live or do things. Sometimes people with the same race don't have the same skin color or culture.

Sometimes people with the same race look similar and have the same culture. Sometimes they don't.

What is **racism**? Racism is when someone is treated badly or differently because of their race or ethnicity.

Racism is not okay. Racism started in the past, but it still happens today.

Sometimes people do racist things, like make fun of someone because of their skin color. This is wrong.

This kind of racism might be easy to spot.

Research shows that bullying someone based on race can affect the person's mental and physical health.

Look!

Look at all these great kids! They are all good friends, and they are all different races. Their races are White, Black, and Mixed. They like to go exploring and play games together.

There are racist acts that are harder to spot, like when kids leave out other kids on purpose because of their race. Sometimes rules can be racist. There can also be racist beliefs about how things are or which things are best. These kinds of racism might be less easy to spot, but they are also wrong.

KIDS AND RACISM

If racism happens to you, it can really hurt. It can be scary and make you worry. You might not be sure if racism has happened to you.

If you did something racist, you might feel bad after. You might worry a lot. You might wonder how to make it better. You could also be confused about why it was wrong.

Make a Guess!

What would the world be like if no one ever stood up to racism? What would it feel like? How would you feel?

If you need help dealing with or thinking about racism, you can talk with someone you trust. This can be a family member, teacher, or friend. It's okay if it feels hard to talk about. There are people who can understand and help.

Even kids can help stop racism. One way to stop racism is by being anti-racist.

Listening to and trying to understand the feelings of people of different races is a great place to start being anti-racist.

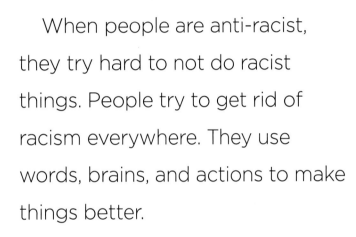

Ask Questions!

You can ask your family and teachers if they've ever spotted something racist. How did they know it was racist? What did they learn?

When people are anti-racist, they try hard to not do racist things. People try to get rid of racism everywhere. They use words, brains, and actions to make things better.

They might stand up for a friend or for themselves. They might speak up if they see something racist in a book. They fix it when they do something wrong.

Racism can be found in a lot of places. The world won't get fixed all in one day. It will take time. Sometimes people will make mistakes as they try to be anti-racist. It's important to keep trying, even when it feels hard.

How can you work together with others to fight against racism?

15

How can you help someone feel they're not alone if they experience racism?

WHAT'S MOST IMPORTANT TO REMEMBER?

Racism happens to kids. Racism is real and wrong, even if some people cannot see it. Racism can really hurt. If racism has happened to you, you are not alone.

Think!

What would you say to someone who was treating another kid unfairly because of their race? Who could you ask for help?

Kids can help stop racism. Everyone can find ways to help people feel safe and loved. If someone does something racist, they have to fix it. The world needs kids to be anti-racist.

If something is racist, we need to fix it.

Diversity helps people be more creative. We can think of solutions for racism together.

REFLECTING ABOUT RACISM

It's important not to make assumptions about someone's race or ethnicity based on how they look. If someone wants to talk about their race, they will.

What is something you would like grown-ups to do to be anti-racist at your school?

What do you want people to understand about racism? What is something you would like your friends to do to be more anti-racist?

How can you work in your community to fight against racism?

Create!

Come up with a plan with friends for what you can do to be anti-racist in your own school and community. You can learn about anti-racism leaders. You can find how they make the world a fairer place.

GLOSSARY

anti-racist (AN-tye RAY-sist) against racism

culture (KUHL-chuhr) beliefs, social norms, and values of a group of people

ethnicity (eth-NIH-suh-tee) a word that can describe a person's heritage, culture, and/or national identity

race (RAYS) group that people can be divided into based on physical characteristics, ethnicity, or shared heritage

racism (RAY-sih-zuhm) unfair and harmful thoughts, beliefs, or actions about someone because of their race

LEARN MORE

Book: *How Can I be an Ally?* By Fatima D. El-Mekki and Kelisa Wing
https://cherrylakepublishing.com/shop/show/52613

Book Series: *Anti-Bias Learning: Social Justice in Action* by various authors
https://cherrylakepublishing.com/shop/show/52686

Video: Sesame Street "What is Racism?" (2020; ~2 min):
https://www.youtube.com/watch?v=XopxsSdecbc

Video: PBS KIDS Talk about Race & Racism (2020; ~28 min): https://www.
youtube.com/watch?v=_fbQBKwdWPg

INDEX

ABOUT THE AUTHORS

AnneMarie K. McClain is an educator, researcher, and parent. Her work is about how kids and families can feel good about who they are. She especially loves finding ways to help kids and families feel seen in TV and books.

Lacey J. Hilliard is a college professor, researcher, and parent. Her work is in understanding how grown-ups talk to children about the world around them. She particularly likes hearing what kids have to say about things.